On the Bus

By James Edward
Character illustrations by Jon Stuart

📖 READ

This book is about a trip to the shops.

When you go to the shops, how do you get there? By car, on foot, by bike or on a bus?

Tiger and his dad are going to the shops. They are going on a bus.

💬 TALK

- Talk with children about how they get to school or to the shops. Why do they travel in this way?

👥 ACTIVITY

- **Have some fun!** Make a chart of the different sort of places children go and how they get there.

Tiger and Dad
go on a bus.

📖 READ

On Saturdays Tiger helps Dad with the shopping.

They go to town by bus, but today they are late!

Tiger runs ahead to wave for the driver to stop.

💬 TALK

- Ask children how they know where a bus is going and which bus to get on.
- How does a bus driver know when to stop for passengers?

👥 ACTIVITY

- Point to the words *huff* and *puff* and ask children to sound-talk them (e.g. huff becomes h-u-ff).
- Then ask them to blend the sounds together and say the words (e.g. h-u-ff becomes huff).

✹ Tip

See the inside back cover for more guidance on sounds.

Stop the bus!

📖 READ

Dad and Tiger get a ride into town on the bus.

When they get close to where they want to get off, Tiger pushes the bell. The bus pulls in at a bus stop.

The door opens. Dad and Tiger get off.

💬 TALK

- Ask children what sound the bus doors will make as they open.
- Ask children to point to the word *hiss*.
- What other sounds do they think Tiger might hear as he gets off the bus (e.g. the bell, the engine rumbling)?

hiss

Tiger and his dad hold hands.

📖 READ

When Dad and Tiger get to the shops, Dad gets out a shopping list.

Together, they collect all the things on the list.

Tiger tries to sneak some more things into the trolley, but Dad spots him!

💬 TALK

- Ask children if they ever help with the shopping. What sorts of things do they get?

👥 ACTIVITY

- **Have some fun!** Ask children to imagine they are going on a shopping trip. Get them to draw five things that they need to buy.

READ

Tiger helps Dad put the shopping on the conveyor belt.

The lady scans all the prices of the shopping into the till.

Dad pays the lady. Tiger puts all the shopping in the shopping bag.

ACTIVITY

- Point to the word *till* and ask children to sound-talk it (i.e. till becomes t-i-ll).
- Then ask them to blend the sounds together and say the word (i.e. t-i-ll becomes till).
- Repeat the activity with the word *fill*.
- What do children notice about the two words? Can they think of any other words that sound like *till* and *fill*?

It's time to go home!

Dad and Tiger wait at the bus stop.

Tiger's dad has bought Tiger an ice lolly to say thank you for helping. He has to eat it before he gets on the bus!

bus stop

No mess on the bus!

I lick it.